This book belongs to
_____

Sara Blakely

By Mary Nhin

Illustrated By
Yuliia Zolotova

This book is dedicated to my children - Mikey, Kobe, and Jojo.

Copyright © 2022 by Grow Grit Press LLC. All rights reserved. No part of this book may be reproduced in any form without permission in writing from the publisher. Please send bulk order requests to growgritpress@gmail.com 978-1-63731-332-9 Printed and bound in the USA. MiniMovers.tv

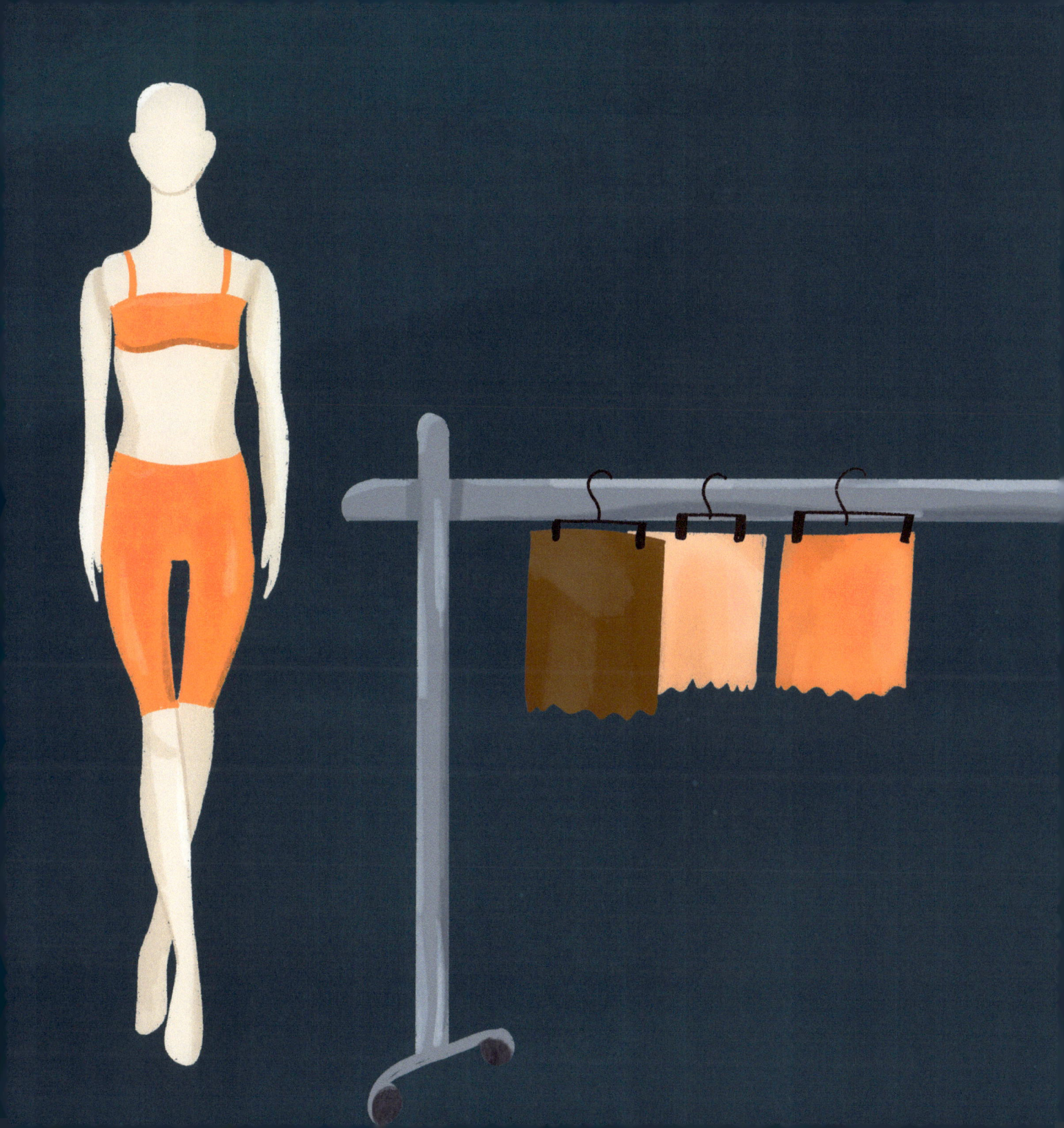

When I was a child, I was encouraged to fail. During dinnertime, while it was common for families to talk about the day's achievements, my father did the opposite. He would ask us what we failed at.

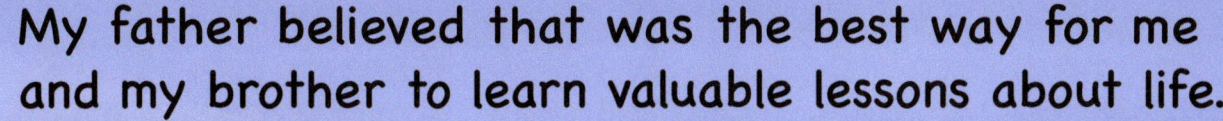

My father believed that was the best way for me and my brother to learn valuable lessons about life.

So what did you try and fail at today?

Yeah! I tried a new thing today, Dad!

Instead of failure being the outcome, failure became not trying. And it forced me at a young age to want to push myself so much further out of my comfort zone. The gift my father gave us was by redefining what failure truly meant.

Growing up, I wanted to be just like my dad, an attorney. But when I failed the entrance exam to study law, I decided on a different path.

Eventually, I took a sales job that involved going from building to building telling people about fax machines. I got used to many rejections, but some people also said yes.

Panel 1:
"Would you like to buy one?"
"No."

Panel 2:
"Would you like to buy one?"
"Yes, thank you."

The job was in Florida and it required me to wear pantyhose. As you can imagine, some days the temperature got so high, I became very, very hot! I often struggled to stay looking professional without overheating.

The worst part about the pantyhose was the seam at the toe. It would look silly when I wore open-toe sandals. So I devised a solution to cut the toe part, but then the pantyhose would ride up my leg.

All of this helped me form an idea for shaping apparel.

I took this idea to the companies that made the hosiery. All the bosses were men, so they didn't understand what it was like to wear their products. In the end, they weren't interested in my idea.

I was disappointed at being rejected, but I knew that my idea was a good one. I decided their rejection was only a minor setback. My parents had prepared me for this moment. I would not be deterred.

Trying new things and not being afraid to fail along the way are more important than what you learn in school.

I decided to research and develop the idea myself, testing the prototypes with my family and friends. I decided on the name Spanx, for my company. It took a lot of time, work, and money.

Finally after two years, a hosiery mill operator agreed to support my idea. I was so happy!

Panel 1:
- "Hi!"
- "Hi Sara, I talked to my three daughters and they really want me to explore your idea."

Panel 2:
- "Thank you so much! I am so grateful!"

I soon learned the real work was persuading the decision makers to sell my products in their stores.

When I finally secured a meeting with a high-end retailer, Neiman Marcus, I decided it was now or never to wow the retail buyer. I quickly changed into the pantyhose in the dressing room and showed her the benefits of my innovation.

I kept working hard, and eventually I got there. With my products on the shelves, sales sky-rocketed!

The products I sold were so popular that I sold millions of dollars in just my first year of business.

1st year sales — $4 million

2nd years sales $10 million

Don't be intimidated by what you don't know. That can be your greatest strength and ensure that you do things differently from everyone else.

Timeline

1998 – Sara's idea is rejected my all the hosiery companies she speaks to

1999 – Sara sells her product as a one-woman business, doing everything herself

2000 – Sara's product, Spanx, is featured on The Oprah Winfrey Show and sales boom

2012 – Sara becomes the youngest self-made billionaire in the world

minimovers.tv

 @marynhin   @GrowGrit
#minimoversandshakers

 Mary Nhin   Ninja Life Hacks

 Ninja Life Hacks

 @ninjalifehacks.tv

www.ingramcontent.com/pod-product-compliance
Lightning Source LLC
Chambersburg PA
CBHW041521070526
44585CB00002B/34